All About
Kangaroos

EDventure
LEARNING

How to Use This Book

This book is part of our Read Together series, a collection of books designed to be enjoyed by a young reader paired with a more experienced reader, such as a parent, grandparent, or older sibling. Take turns reading out loud together.

The pages on the left side are meant for the younger reader. These pages use short, simple sentences and larger print. They are marked at the bottom of the page with the symbol shown at left.

The right-side pages are for the older reader. They contain paragraphs with longer sentences and more complex vocabulary. These pages are marked at the bottom of the page with the symbol shown at right.

Shared reading helps new readers gain confidence. It's also a great way for all ages to bond over books. We hope you enjoy this book as you Read Together.

Copyright © 2020 by EDventure Learning LLC

All rights reserved. This book or any portion thereof may not be reproduced or used in any manner whatsoever without the express written permission of the publisher.

Printed in the United States of America
Paperback ISBN: 978-1-64824-013-3

EDventure Learning LLC
5601 State Route 31 #1296
Clay, NY 13039

www.edventurelearning.com
Email us at hello@edventurelearning.com

Table of Contents

What Kangaroos Look Like .... p. 4

Where Kangaroos Live .... p. 14

What Kangaroos Do .... p. 20

Glossary .... p. 28

Index and Credits .... p. 29

What Kangaroos Look Like

They stand on two legs.

Kangaroos stand upright on their two long, strong back legs. Their huge feet help them hop.

They have short fur.

Kangaroos are covered in short, thick fur that is either red, brown, or grey. Some kangaroos also have white fur on their bellies.

They have big tails.

A kangaroo's tail is nearly as long as the rest of its body. It is thick and muscular. It helps the kangaroo to balance.

Kangaroo moms have pouches.

Kangaroos are **marsupials**- animals that grow inside pouches. Only female kangaroos have pouches. These pockets on the front of the body are used to carry baby kangaroos, called **joeys**.

Joeys are born blind, hairless, and less than an inch long. They crawl into the pouch and stay there while they grow. Joeys may stay in their mothers' pouches for over a year.

Kangaroos are tall and heavy.

Joeys may start out tiny, but they grow up to be huge! Kangaroos are the world's largest marsupials. There are four kinds of kangaroo. The largest is the red kangaroo, which stands around 5-6 feet (1.5-1.8 m) tall and weighs up to 200 pounds (90.7 kg). Only slightly smaller are the eastern and western grey kangaroos and the antilopine kangaroos. In all species, males are larger than females.

Where Kangaroos Live

All wild kangaroos live in one part of the world.

Kangaroos are native to Australia. Different species of kangaroos can be found all over the continent and its surrounding islands.

Some live on dry plains.

Red kangaroos live in dry areas throughout Australia. They mostly live on open, grassy plains but may also live in deserts or in thinly wooded areas.

Some live in the forest.

Both eastern and western grey kangaroos live in wooded areas in the southern part of the continent. Antilopine kangaroos live in the tropical forests of northern Australia.

What Kangaroos Do

They hop.

Kangaroos are the only large animals that use hopping as their main way to get around. They actually cannot walk upright because of the shape of their legs.

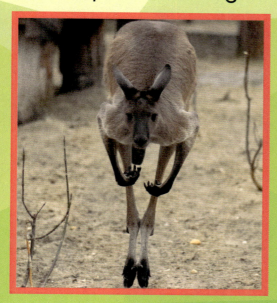

Kangaroos can hop far and fast. A red kangaroo can hop 25 feet (7.6 m) in one jump and can reach speeds of 40 miles (64 km) per hour.

They use their tails to "walk."

Kangaroos cannot walk upright, and hopping takes them far and fast. If they want to make smaller, slower movements, they do a strange "walk" that uses all four legs and their tails. They bend over so that all four legs are on the ground. They walk their front legs forward. Then, they balance on their front legs and tail while lifting both back legs together and swinging them forward. This is how kangaroos move when they are eating.

They eat plants.

Kangaroos are **herbivores**, which means they only eat plants. They mostly eat grass but will also make a meal of flowers, fruit, and moss.

They live in groups.

A group of kangaroos is called a **mob**. A mob can be as small as 10 kangaroos or as large as over 100.

Glossary

Herbivore

Animal that eats only plants

Joey

Baby kangaroo

Marsupial

Animal that develops inside a pouch on its mother's body

Mob

A group of kangaroos

Index

A
Appearance, 4-7, 10-13
Antilopine kangaroo, 13, 19
Australia, 15, 17, 19

F
Food, 24-25

G
Grey kangaroo (eastern and western), 13, 19

H
Habitat, 14-19

J
Joey, 11, 13

M
Marsupial, 11
Mob, 27
Movement, 5, 20-23

R
Red kangaroo, 13, 17, 21

Credits

The images in this book are used with permission as follows. Images not listed here are © EDventure Learning LLC.

Cover and title page: Pen Ash | Pixabay; Interior backgrounds: Kappy Kappy | Rawpixel; p. 3: Angello | Pexels; p. 4: Holger Link | Unsplash; p. 5: Pen Ash | Pixabay; p. 6: Philippe Oursel | Unsplash; p. 7: Sipa | Pixabay; p. 8: Pen Ash | Pixabay; p. 9: Janeb13 | Pixabay; p. 10: John Torcasio | Unsplash; p. 11: Ethan Brooke | Pexels; p. 12: Holger Detje | Pixabay; p. 13: Elena Svetleyshaya | Dreamstime (left), Macrovector | Freepik (right); p. 14: Titus Staunton | Pixabay; p. 15: Clker Free Vector Images | Pixabay (top), Moerschy | Pixabay (bottom); p. 16: William Christen | Unsplash; p. 17: Skeeze | Pixabay; p. 18: Mark Galer | Unsplash; p. 19: The Mind Fellows | Unsplash; p. 20: Ashish Upadhyay | Unsplash; p. 21: Suzuha Kozuki | Unsplash (top), Holdosi | Pixabay (bottom); p. 22: Terri Sharp | Pixabay; p. 23: Public Domain Pictures | Pixabay (top), Pixabay (bottom); p. 24: Marcus Byrne | Unsplash; p. 25: Andreas Schau | Pixabay (top), Alexas Fotos | Pixabay (bottom); p. 26: Carles Rabada | Unsplash; p. 27: Tony Media | Pixabay; p. 28 (from top): Marcus Byrne | Unsplash, Ethan Brooke | Pexels, John Torcasio | Unsplash, Tony Media | Pixabay

Check out these other titles in the Read Together series!

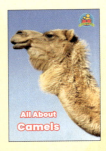 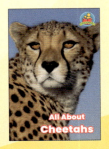 

All About Camels   All About Cheetahs   All About Giraffes

All About Elephants   All About Kangaroos

Keep in touch!

FOLLOW US ON SOCIAL MEDIA

   @edventurelearning

 www.edventurelearning.com

 Want freebies? Email us at **hello@edventurelearning.com** with the subject "Read Together" to join our newsletter and we'll send you free printables to keep the learning going!

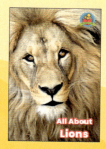

All About Lions

All About Penguins

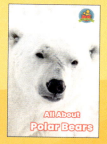

All About Polar Bears

All About Tigers

All About Zebras

Made in the USA
Monee, IL
12 January 2024